IN THE OPEN

For Jaime —
whose generous spirit
echoes his mother's —
thank you for sharing
your poems &
likewise here for you —
love
Bee

8/18/98

Also by Beatrix Gates

native tongue

Shooting at Night

The Wild Good:
Lesbian Photographs and Writings on Love, editor

IN
THE
OPEN

BEATRIX
GATES

POEMS

PAINTED LEAF PRESS

NEW YORK CITY

Copyright © 1998   Beatrix Gates
Book design, production and cover montage: John Masterson
Cover photograph: Beatrix Gates
Author photo: Becket Logan

Library of Congress Cataloging-in-Publication Data
Gates, Beatrix
      In the Open / Beatrix Gates.--1st ed.
         p.   cm.
      ISBN: 0-9651558-7-0 (alk. paper)
      I. Title.
    PS3557. A86815 1998
    811' .54--dc21   97-45799
                                            CIP

Printed in the United States of America
Painted Leaf Press,
P.O. Box 2480 Times Square Station,
New York, New York 10108-2030
First Edition
10 9 8 7 6 5 4 3 2 1

for Jane Cooper

&

for Jean Valentine

Acknowledgments

Grateful acknowledgment goes to the editors of the following publications where some of these poems, several in different versions, first appeared: *Blue Unicorn; The Kenyon Review (Theatre Issue); The Long Story; Newsletter/Center for the Study of Women and Society* (City University of New York, Graduate School); *Nimrod; The North Dakota Quarterly; OutWeek; Ripenings: Sing Heavenly Muse!; The Sarah Lawrence Literary Review; Sinister Wisdom; Sojourner; The Women's Review of Books* and *Yellow Silk.*

Thanks also go to the editors of the following anthologies in which these poems appeared: "Deadly Weapon" in *Gay & Lesbian Poetry in Our Time,* eds. Morse and Larkin, St. Martin's; "I wrap myself" and "Conversations with the Body" in *Naming the Waves,* ed. McEwen, Crossing Press and Virago; "Montage" in *queer city*: The Portable Lower East Side, eds. Robinson, Romo-Carmona, Silverberg & Woodson; "Dream: Bay Foal" in *The Key to Everything,* ed. Pearlberg, St. Martin's; "Carol" (from "Triptych) in *The Arc of Love,* ed. Coss, Scribner's; "Refuge" (section III) in *The Zenith of Desire,* ed. Pearlberg, Crown; "Pond" (as "Sonnet") in *My Lover Is a Woman,* ed. Newman, Ballantine Books; and "Homeless" (from "Triptych") in *Things Shaped in Passing,* More "Poets for Life": Writing from the AIDS Pandemic, eds. Klein & McCann, Persea Books. "Esprit de Corps" appeared in my chapbook *Shooting at Night,* Granite Press and "Q.E.II-Bermuda to New York" in a letterpress limited edition, *Q.E.II-Bermuda to New York/Gunbeat,* collaboration with Meredith Stricker, San Francisco. The excerpt from *Breaking Open* by Muriel Rukeyser is reprinted by generous permission of Bill Rukeyser.

Particular appreciation goes to the Cummington Community of the Arts, The MacDowell Colony, The Millay Colony, The Vermont Studio Center, The Virginia Center for the Creative Arts, and Ann Stokes at Welcome Hill for providing time and space in which to write. I would also like to thank Eva Kollisch as well as Betsy Crowell and Louise Fishman for offering me quiet places to work.

For insight, enduring support, and critical encouragement, I would like to thank Electa Arenal, Jane Cooper, Anne Dembska, Andrea Hawks, Eva Kollisch, Rosa Lane, Joan Larkin, Jan Heller Levi, Thomas Lux, Jaime Manrique, Cassandra Medley, Jay Meek, Bob Nichols, Diana O'Hehir, Sharon Olds, Grace Paley, Roz Parr, Marie Ponsot, Martha Ramsey, Naomi Replansky, Bessy Reyna, Barbara Smith, and Jean Valentine as well as Nancy Nowak, Leslie Chatterton and Victoria Hallerman. I am also grateful to John Masterson for his sensitive eye and hand and to Bill Sullivan for his commitment to the work.

Note: ~ indicates stanza break

CONTENTS

" The collective unconscious is the living history brought to the present in consciousness, waking or sleeping. The personal 'unconscious' is the personal history... In facing history, we look at each other, and in facing our entire personal life, we look at each other."
                    —Muriel Rukeyser from *Breaking Open*

I

CUT SCENES
for David

Call your brother home
Slowly say the bones.

I wake in the night— blossom,
no leaf. I am falling, yes, this is
the random float of beauty, full
veins of color detached from the tree,
the air capable of all things.

I wake in the fullness
of my still untethered past, body
whirling on my bones   praying to be let down
on the ground where I can walk away.

I am not dreaming, run
to the trees around my house—
quick up to branches, bark
lined on my cheek. Inside, face
against storm windows, I watch
the blue-gray print of breath disappear,
open the awkward aluminum frame.
Huge flakes pour in. I smell the cold's large holes
in the room— my hunger for raw elements
meeting the hunger of the cold.

I have sought the structure of the house—
studied blue in the foundation,
warm in the wood, the bright string of rooms—
to bury the sounds of humiliation,
quiet fire at the end of the corridor.

The doors change rooms, the windows
give on the same world: this we
that choked, entangled: mother/father
dying for a long time,
and two last ones, afloat in the nightmare we,
learning to fly by walking on the ground.

BOTTLENECK

I am the driver in the dark red
car. Flagman sprouts emergency
from his hands. Fingers close
around my neck, my constant leaning forward
over the wheel into injury.
I slow as the light blinks caution—
memory waving from my skull,
red against the glass...

one: my bones lie down, liquid in the shadow
         of the boyman who kneels on my arms
         and tames my neck in his hands.

two: red, red   no   red turns purple
         when red shaggy breath
         child cries   blue   sky above me.

three: my head is a paper bag.

four: my head is a helmet
         with words in it.

five: I cut my neck
         myself in an experiment.
         I want the cool glass
         on my skin and never imagine it will break,
         my bottleneck. They do not know we
         did it together. I took the glass
         in my hand when he said take it
         and ran the edge against my beating skin.
         I learn that I show. Embarrassed
         and proud, I reveal the wound.
         It speaks to them and they bandage it up.
         The family doctor speaks about the biggest vein
         and how lucky I was.
         Now I know just what to do
         when I want to.

DREAM: WOMEN'S ACTION

We have been seen. We are important or perhaps we are in the important area where the central ones are being transported. We are added to the bus and taken to the institutional building with the other women. The side opens. It looks like one of the truck entrances to the Pentagon. Isn't there a subway under here? Whose cars are those in the parking lot? This is a border. Are we near Canada, the woods thick on the horizon. Vermont, upstate New York, Canada. That's it. I

Inside, I am relieved it is a hospital, not a prison. I can breathe, then remember a hospital means our bodies are under suspicion. My relief is only as long as my next breath. There is the silent comfort of the others. We have beds in the same large corner room. I am a little comforted. I lie down and promise not to touch my feet to the floor. This is the first rule I've heard.

I have a doctor who is called mine. I am thinking he will not hurt me. He doesn't look as if it's his fault he's here. I am forgiving him, and I turn on my stomach. He climbs on top of me and lies perfectly still. I sink under his weight without a sound. You might not know I am there, under him, his out-line so perfectly traces mine. Somehow, his body has been fed the information, the x-rays, and he has adapted the contours of his body to fit my bones. He is becoming a shadow of me. I am there and he is not. He wears light poplin and I am sheeted white. I am thinking of what the others will say, but I can't see them, I am so deep in my mattress. Quite suddenly, we are all up, hastened to inspect our quarters. There are large open windows. I know I can escape, the roof an easy drop. At the same moment, I realize no bars are needed. Every thought of escape is reversing itself into the destruction of our connectedness. They have turned the power of dreaming against us. I know I cannot live without my imagination.

My mother's brother enters and I remember he worked for Eisenhower before he opened his head on a stone wall deep in the Virginia woods. He looks down as if charged with a difficult duty. He is dressed in pale browns and looks soft. He announces in a quiet voice that he's made a mistake. There are eleven of us and only five may survive. There can be poison in the food at unan-nounced intervals. It doesn't matter which six go. In fact, we can choose. Pistols may be given on request, one chamber loaded, and supervision.

My uncle says he's sorry, but it can't be helped. I scream No, striking at his face and chest, my arms aching from the blows. He does not try to protect himself, some acknowledgment of the injustice I think, then realize my blows leave no new marks. I see only the scar he carries from boyhood darkening in a diago-nal along his cheek, the place where his fears bind, quickly sealing the cut: a boy, a bottle, a rocky beach and the glass through his cheek. The scar would be the premonition of his death: falling forward onto the stone wall as he looked for the short cut to town in the blizzard. He sought his wife and young daughter who had moved soon after he began slitting the tires. He cut in a diagonal along the smooth insides of the studded snow tires, his pulse beating hard in his hands and feet, the whiskey heat.

He found no way past the stone wall.

I look deeply into his face and know I have learned the same ways: how to drink and drive off the ones I love. I know how to make a wall my death. This is the closest we will get, he and I, this breath of loss between us. I reach for the women. He has given me valuable information, no protection.

DEADLY WEAPON

for Leslie, Rosa & Margaret who were there, 1981
and in memory of Charlie Howard, gay man murdered in Bangor, 1984

We came home to the stranger:
Scarsdale. The move to the city
still rattling at our backs, even our shadows ran
thin as threads, then wide as plates.
We blinked at the walls, their whiteness,
and moved furniture into comforting positions.
This night, we drove with country
determination— two women in a car
no one could see under the flowing sheet of rain.
Unused to locks, we lost
both sets of keys and had to break in,
then laughed, got out the smoke
and curled tight on the bed. Hot wind
blew hissing through the screen,
open window.

I lay naked on top of the sheets,
the green comforter slipped again
to the floor and your remaining clothing.
You turned the pages of your magazine—
lazily licking your fingers,
toking on the joint and gently slapping
the pages. "Making the scene
with a magazine," I leaned on your turning
arm and fell back, liking to be fed
tokes in a continuum. The dog pressed his chest
against the cardboard boxes collapsing
the sides, straining to get to the window, his nose
pointing to the open screen.
"Come here, Lou, out of the boxes."
The buzzer rang. We scowled at each other
and as you pulled on your jeans, you asked the door,
"Who is it?" The pounding, fisted, began a loud,
dull hammer over the rain.

Sweatpants by the bed, I slip
them on, turn for a shirt, a top, something.
Through the heat, it is the sound
of speed, a hissing splits the room. It feels just

like I've dreamt so often— dreaming of wars,
I am shot again and again, feel the burn
of bullets, the burn of being
alive is wondrous and strange.
I moan and drop by the bed, listen
to the crunch of sand on the floor by my shoes.
I see the short, yellow arrow,
stand up and hurl it at the window.
My hands do not have the power
of the triggered crossbow and the arrow
falls a dizzy, harmless end-over-end.
"You fuckhead, get the fuck out of here."
Scream at the waiting window
as you run between me and the opening,
snap off the light.

We move to the center room—
no windows here, fumble for the phone,
knock it to the floor. *What's our address*
remembering our apartment has no number,
but letters like signals. You collect the phone
in your hands, dial the police
through the operator. I am full of violence
and hold my thigh tightly, both hands,
wide as nets, look down, feel the blood
hot and sticky. Squeeze tighter. They ask,
"Is anyone wounded?" "No, no, Yes, yes
one of us has been hit." Hang up. "They're coming."
"Who cares, I wish I had a gun to blast
the windows, blow his face off."
The dog presses to my knees
under the table and you lean close,
"we've both been wounded."

You call Rosa and Margaret, call to say
what? "Something terrible has happened."
and you make the words work with your tears.
"We need you to come,
Yes, now. We're
all right. We need you." Hang up.
We look at each other, know we are seeing
in the dark, our chairs click
against each other, old bones, close,

chosen. We cannot touch and our bodies
have put on the weighted coat, the lie.
We have already moved to the inner lining
in the center of the apartment where we can't be
seen. We breathe together, rattling the mix
of hate and fear, blood in the air
and nested somewhere safe outside.
This is what the arrow wanted—
to strike us apart. The blue lights
flash at the edges of the shades
as we take each other's hands appearing
and disappearing before our eyes.

Two detectives question us. Six policemen stand around
the front room, arms moving, radios loud.
They are angry and talk to each other, unbelieving.
"In Scarsdale, who'd shoot two girls in Scarsdale?
With a crossbow? That's a long-range, deadly weapon."
You are the girl visiting. This they make up
themselves, unable to picture us in bed. We said we were
both in the bedroom. The medic escorts me into the bathroom,
"to have a look." I hear them ask you if you turned down
any guys recently, in a bar, anything like that.
"Easy now, pull down your pants, so I can see."
His hands turn my leg. I am miles away, can't believe
this man is touching me. The last question:
"Do you have any enemies?"

The nurse shows me the examining room,
pulls back the curtain. "Just one of you
can come." Rosa is holding you
knowing to touch. The curtain closes. Margaret
takes my hands. I see the nurse's calves
and white shoes leave. "Let yourself cry," Margaret tells me,
"I know how strong you are. You don't have to
be strong now." I hear my mother speaking
as she puts her arms around my neck—
one day in her dying she broke
and pulled me close, cried against my chest,
I can't be strong all the time.
Just once. I let the shot come up, a hailstone
in my throat. The nurse returns,
"What's the matter honey?

It's all over now."

No one can come with me
to be x-rayed— and it is the x-ray technician
who suggests I have been shot by Westchester's own
Dart Man. "I don't think they ever caught him.
The publicity died down, what with Son of Sam.
I never heard anymore." He pins me
in position, hip hard against the machine, drapes the gray
radiation shield across the top of my body.
I turn my face as he enters his protected booth.
I haven't been in a hospital
since I kissed my dead mother's forehead
goodbye in May. She had wanted
radiation. And it was her doctor, a young
man, who told her it wouldn't help.
Somehow, she believed him— like no other.
I've lost all modesty, she said and gave herself
to the cure, injections of platinum that searched
and searched her veins for a way
out. This most precious metal, white
gold, shone in her veins
like belief.

A man ran from our window
leaving his imprint in the mud—
the footprints filled with water, the definition
slurred as the ground gave way.
He is the one who saw
us, did not deny his vision, picked up
the closest weapon, aimed and fired.
There have been others, more
usual. My mother worked to keep
us apart, speaking to you
only when I was in the room,
when she felt she had to, that last Christmas
at home. Alone for a moment, she would always ask
you the same question: *When are you leaving,
what bus, what train, when did you say
you were going?* She refused to enter any house
we shared and when we thought she would
we moved all the furniture of her imagination
for her— the extra bed, the live example of our

separateness. So she stood at the door,
This isn't as bad as I thought and we knew
we had imagined well— taken on her mask
for our own and forced her to bless our lie.
There was nothing right for her
about you. When she died, you were the first
to ask, "When are you coming home?"

September 1981- 87

SPARKS STREET

Mother, all your relatives are dead,
the ones we had to memorize
staring down the stories
and plates of glass, the dinners
we took to heart and slept with.
My head creased the pillows
and wore the perfunctory blue
of your goodnight kiss.

The dead still wait, dog
the doors, whites of the eyes
rolled up like a sleeve of moon
hanging in the atmosphere.
This is called memory
when the live ones leave,
grow out through the latches
and hold onto the keys.

Loose with banging, heavy
with inside fury, the house
was sold. The stories stayed
in our heads, sure as winter
and the late, ungiving March wind.
Our eyes smarted in the cold.

My hands set like carved attachments
on the arms of the chair.
My mind blinking on and off,
I kept being
reminded of motion, struck
like a match, yes!
I could not for the life of me move
but sat and sat in the same chair
inside this, my last house, my home.

FAMILY TREE

The brothers of both generations had a violence in common
as if creating pain was genius,
the pride of the family— a moron
couldn't have done better than Tom,
the eldest and first to roost
at the quick of his quick, caged brain.

He held his sister at bay with an attack
dog— just held the dog back from making strings
of her vocal chords. Let the dog snap. So that
was the story of why my grandmother always wore
a brooch at her throat... the scars like grosgrain ribbon
to my small hands that prodded and adored her,
her with the softest hanging plum of sun-
blue skin just back of her smiling, pointed chin.

George took a knife, armed in broad daylight, got his
sister screaming and stopped her, screaming.
Chased her right out the window and onto the roof,
never once told how it took imagination, though he knew it
as courage. Back inside, he had only to twirl the carving knife
handle in his hand. After all, he was the eldest and the stand-in,
what with father dying way upstairs. It was his duty
to do the carving, the red meat falling slowly
to the platter. *Pass your plate.* And she sat—
first on one hand, then the other— my mother,
keeping her plate in front of her,
bone-white, refusing daughter.

LAWSUIT

for my brother

The bad taste lingers, the fingered
rings and forks and knives. Lives
and spoons lie still haunted, hammered
in the vault. Residual heirs
mete out resentment for nourishment,
greed as common ground.
Why, the very sound of your voice
starts the gnawing up again, hungry
and hungrier; this heartlessness keeps
neediness alive and will not settle
until the court has named the bloodtie
undeserving, bankrupt, wild
seed gone wrong. Survival of the
litigious depends on like-minded
species, so we have set to melting down
the veins, impacted silver in the mountain.
We are tunneling back
into the bloodstream, back to
the natural resources in ourselves.

SUICIDE
for my Uncle Charlie

I begin here— knowledge of ice, stony
ribs, cracked mountain, New England.
Cold playing on the air,
every ray drops a deep shadow—
is it early spring in the mountains,
chill rising from the ground?
An explosion rips the sun's path to the west.
Vibration shakes the air to fiber,
glass that can't be seen through. Distortion.
Compressed into flight: trees, whirl of small stones,
sheared rock, houses, ripped glass— the air slit
and clearly alternating between light and debris.
Still, I thank the earth for my mobile flesh, the muscle
clinging to bone clinging to the earth.
We are in the seam of the explosion.
I did know someone else but who was it?

I don't remember any color, clothing or features—
no sex— just the feel of another,
a human sound as we pressed into softening ground, cold mud
and new bright hairs of grass, islands still holding.
We share a past, both look to the great Scotch pine
and turn to each other as the proud, gray scales of bark
split open into shafts of tan and rosy wood,
gold beads of sap. We remember the names of other
trees, what we've been taught with our hands, the seasons
and this bone-deep fear. We
recognize the nightly screening of a war on T.V.,
torn cities we grew up in. Through cracks all around us,
multiplying divisions come home
to bodies we hide inside, doubled over,
hands to feet, seeking comfort in the breaking
air around us.

CHAINLETTER FROM THE 50'S TO THE 80'S

We are riding in the car, stop
at a large, aluminum mailbox, flag
up. Mum hands me the letter, asks me
to get out and mail it. I take it,
touch the white, sealed envelope
alone. I am sealed in an unknown place,
known only as this place where she lets me go
without warning. I start reading:
As women, we have learned to use each other.
You are of no use to me as you are.
Find others.
and at the bottom,
Do not break the chain.

I have never read this before.
My mother wrote this
with her friends. They are listed
as previous recipients, some daughters included.
This is the familiar welcome: separate hands
greeting abandonment as closest kin.
My bones sharpen under my skin— the torn,
embarrassed and turned away. I want the names
and rip them open. They are of use to me.
They point towards my feet, the ground, make a trail
I can call clear, not beautiful.
Mending these pale roots of shame,
I find others and break
the chain.

DAUGHTER AS MOTHER

Are you coming with me?
I cannot ask any other way. Let's
leave the marked place, home.
It is our own steps, our own movement
that will take us from here.
Remember motion. All that travelling
away— this time it's yours.
It's here within reach if you could
reach— were we ever the same
age, and how will I know?

There was the photograph outside
your own house, same town. Your mother gave
it to me, asking *Who is this? It's me,* I answered.
And it was you silent this time in the photo...
shoulders turned in and out at the same time
like clipped wings, hands closed, arms flat
and hair clipped back. You looked as if you had been
let out by mistake, ill-at-ease outdoors.

Now the light and space are gone, life outgrown
entirely. I can see you.
We have been turned against each other
so long, I am shocked,
adrift in these rays.

Are you coming with me? Let's leave this
marked place— indelible, invisible,
the place where you hinged all
your hope and displaced, violent,
took to separate corners.
I met your unrelenting fury
full-face— the rest became atmospheric
pressure of moods, your faces roamed the hall
vying for space. The surviving
words, *Leave me, Leave me alone.*
These are the places where we
give it up. The dust-cleared corners
at the edge of empty space.

When I am small, I find places. I flatten
myself along the shelves for hours— rough, dry towels

and pale blue blankets. These are my comforters.
Coats too. Coats that pile up like warm
bodies as the cocktail party din rises.
You are free tonight and will go
dancing. I am safe in the sleeve of a fur
curled and sleeping. If I cannot go
with you, I can be close. These smells
that make you happy. I am deep inside
the cast-off warmth, the swirling
cool of gin's perfume
breathing with my mouth open.

THE NINTH WAVE
for Jane

I am driving on the death road   saying no
shaking the snake in front of me:
I have been afraid
ride the yellow line, the road
a coal twist in the distance.
I have learned never to turn
my back on water. The wave's split
foam darkens the sand as I scan
the muscling surface for the ninth wave.

Without listening, I hear my mind
stutter across the death landscape—
New England houses stretched and shrunken
They are houses without family
and they were houses without welcome.
I lived in a shame box
kept my ear to the wall as you worked
the pale oak floorboards   rays under my door.
The names you called me
gathered   a herd of animals
scanning doors for light and hope of quiet.

The salt air carves close: apple limbs
greening at the tips   distance
to the coming season quickly taken in
and judged. I have sat here
and not known which way to turn. Roots
I do not want have been cut away:
underground rooms soften, haunt.

I cannot imagine laughter:
slightly rounded screens,
thrown-open windows. To feel
my own need no longer tight under my skin,
and the power of what was taken— the guard
of quiet and constantly melting will,
no longer the absent-minded air around me.

I am headed to my mother's house,
have stopped waiting for death to leave.
She is dead and lives there.

Tears welcome me— my constellation of bright scars.
Ribs spring strong around my heart,
long pulls of air.

II

HAWK

I

Your eyes on a moving target:
perhaps a mouse, muted brown near
the roots of the pale lined grasses.

Diving: eyes red as Mars
depth-charge the air.
Feet lace, cage the swirling fur.

I know you never lie— there is no place
safe from your constant curiosity.
You are all intention,

while outside your field of sight—
denial, the form you inherited as focus,
the form your wings take daily

to resist and funnel the wind.
You are the only one who attacks
in flight. Nothing escapes you.

II

And today, the accidental—
something without direction
like hope or chance— your life turned perfect

by uncritical surprise. Here you are—
chest up, road under open wings. Eyes shine,
red pearls over the heart, on gray and brown feathers.

Somehow you have landed here—
faultless on the ordinary pavement.
No one has touched you.

What a vision it must've been!
Spitfire, your eyes
rolled around the bone-hard world

of your skull and into the atmosphere.
Brilliant and small, you wore your pride—
dangling, busted, home.

MAY 14, 1980
in memory, Clare Haskins Gates

You gestured *Up*, the morning here for you at last
and busied your body with putting out your fever's fire,
found coals fit for one more day. Making the bed around the body
I make my words as I go, turn in speechless corners; your piece
of the conversation, a clear blue glassy look, sky between us, separation.
You said, *We're going home.* The nurse read deeper into the paper.

Death slipped between us, tactile, all-of-a-piece
and pulsed my life-dry leaves on fire.
One-sided touch, my hands burn in the air, last
to let go, falling in the wax light of the room. Your face, a paper-
thin mute wrapping. You, too, are outside the body—
no healing this permanent wound of separation.

The lightning sky opens the dark in pieces,
desperate to find itself, the ground, the body
that could no longer hold the familiar, willful fire
lining your face, now crackles, explosive, outside the last
night's breathing. Will this be what I remember, lightning scrawls on blackpaper
or is this escaping from you, the rain, the lightning all-separating?

Black and white, nothing could be clearer, the body
is a mere house and cold at that, separated
from the rest of us here beside you, your last papers.
We bury ourselves in the tasks at hand, the endless pieces
that must relocate into another kind of lasting
or do we give up and throw the words wasted into the fire?

Who are we now? My cheekbones are yours, firing
red and pushing hard under my skin. The embarrassed daughter lasts
to admire the flickering structures of bone embodying
the likeness. Never the same nor now in separation,
my skin still burns easy as paper—
while you, you drove your anger in your heart, in pieces.

I scan the sky, flagged with fire-
boned fingers and let the center go, oh last
word or first to know. I am fresh as blank paper
and say simply: *Go.* Make the separation,
go from us all. I sit now, empty, with the body
and know it is not you. Peace.

~

We write the obituary for the papers and separate
the body from the facts of your life. Burn the body in the fire.
What lasts is the world in pieces.

Q.E. II BERMUDA TO NEW YORK, 1956

We are berthed in Hamilton Harbor
ready to cast off. My eyes just over
the first rail, white pleats and dark trousers
to both sides. Boxed flowers
and yellow envelopes come up the plank
from men in blue suits and caps.
People throw flowers at the ship.
I like this. Then I see we throw something else—
it's money. I dig fast,
get my pennies ready.
Kids from there don't wear tops
and dive for money. My pennies
out of the water, fists high
each time he salutes me.
Again, he tucks his head and goes under.
The engines start, coins
still shiny in the air.
Water churns white and I see the pink
of his mouth opening.
The wake covers his face.
Someone throws a life-saver ring.
He gets on, limbs trailing loose
in the water. They do not scold him
but lay him down, empty his pockets.
Pennies pool around his waist.
His arms and legs spill across the dock,
one coin silver by his head,
his clouding eyes.
He doesn't move, something bad in the money.

My father's absence bright around me,

I took this pale cloak
and learned to disappear.
I waited for him as I thought
he must be waiting in some other room.
His wife cut away at the air
until it sat thick around my feet.
Asleep in his chair by nine,
his silence poured over us.
I said to my head, my hardest
proud part, *it will stop, it will*
stop and I stopped the words
at my neck and ears, stopped
my breath and moved slowly away.

My father read in bed and bathroom,
book propped in his lap, the loose pages
turning further into the story.
I stopped the words in lines
that moaned and flew beyond themselves
into his world of books
and hoped he would stumble on them,
rise from his chair and speak
to me directly. Anger
did not have a room
but had a thirst. We sucked on ice
and drank the knife.

Who are you who I try to love
by osmosis— through walls, always
around her. Mother does not want us
speaking. I forget
I am a child. I forget my father's not.
He is very old, a worn smooth skull
and loses his hearing in larger and larger spaces.
He is a young girl really. He says
he doesn't know what's the matter and apologizes
for making her so upset. It is too late
I know as she begins on him... for lying down
and taking it from the world.
She is the world.

~

When he drove away, a salesman,
he grew small and I knew the pain of it.
He sold instruments of change,
weather and perspective.
I took the binoculars
in my hands many times: touched
the hard leather, green felt
lining, black lens caps.
I focussed on the trees in the yard,
their contribution: how the leaves were lit
from inside. For me, I could blur to change
and always snap out of it:

drop the binoculars and return to the room,
see the deep circles of magnified
sight printed on my face,
the trees wrapping my skull
like friends waving in the background
as I became the silhouette seeking light
against the fading sky.

GETTING THE MESSAGE

I take what you give me, take
the blame. Something is wrong.
I cover myself, make up
answers to the growing
questions. Some call this lying.
I don't know what else to do
to keep up
under my knobby, rolling surface
where everything pours off,
and the repeating— *you'll have to*
figure it out yourself:

I am a pesterer
when I inhabit the same
house. I am in the yard, you want me
hidden, in the living room, dining
room, kitchen, the hall.
I come in, always late,
I bump into things.
Don't I live here?
I devote hours to a plexiglas ocean
in a bottle, the silent back and forth
plashing in my hands. The question grows
out again to the slick rolling surface, rolls back.

The ocean breaks inside my room, inside
the bottle, against the windows
and into the mirrors.
I will not break. You will never know anything
about me, including how much I hate.
This is how we find our likeness,
at home in this battle, pass it on.

My eyes scan for weakness. I want to make you
stand alone, shadowless. I want to kill
the one you deny exists,
the one like me. I will die
companion for the child you never were,
be your bruised face. I will do it
for you and your hate will love me.
I will never get out and you

will never get in: I will be protected
and so will you. It is love
that cannot
enter freely.

NATURAL ENEMIES

I

Thanksgiving, a family gathers
to eat together. It is country,
by the sea— room enough
to run outside after the meal,
the air sharp, breath short,
hot as the moments held inside.

We shake hands around the room,
the extras stand, look down
at my ruffled hair which never stays
but runs like loose shiny film
around the room. My cousins come down-
stairs. I am told they have been waiting
all day to see me. The eldest catches
me with his first glance, hair
switches across my eyes.

His bulk fills the stairs, his hands
flash in front of him, come down the railing.
His hands take my hands, fling me out into the room,
a hearty laugh. This is what they will call *darling*.
I must hold on to these hands. The room whirls
around me. I am spinning away into the air.
It is the beginning of the anaesthesia.
This is supposed to be what I love.
Let me down I am praying
with my separated hands.
Let me down to the ground.

His mother laughs and tells the room
how well we get along, *and over twelve years between them.*
He is their size but I do not think
he is a grown-up. His hands take my face, touch
my bones, *How beautiful you will be.* I pray with separated
eyes for ugliness, for not seeing, for not looking
in the same direction— anything not to see as he does.
His largest hand covers my head, my blond hair thins
under it. His smallest, fastest hand runs between my legs.
I fold up and wing my way away
wishing my blond hair feathered gray and brown,

my body the speed of a bird.

I move to the light, my pale yellow
changing afternoon on the bed of his room.
My legs feel like fists as I make my way
down the stairs. They are having another
round of drinks. I grab my jacket and run
outside to the younger ones whose guns I easily pick up,
the death of imagination and say nothing
really happened.

The tablecloth hems us loosely in,
skirts our knees. These are my cousins, the hated
pale blond dogs and the missing
middle brother who has run away.
This I understand as I face my own
family, scattered, salt and pepper, along the white skirt
of linen. I have been told which chair has been stolen
from which relative's house but I like the new paint on them,
feel myself in the bright shell of hiding, sink
into the colors, the rugs, the paintings. I know how
to get away, steal myself from my own body and slip
out to the light. My family is not there. Not one of them
stays with me. I laugh outloud. They call it
joining in. We are having a feast.

II

If the boys make fun
of me, I will be a monkey
and my lightness will take me
to the smallest, high tip of the tree.
Here I have feet like hands and hands like feet—
I can pull my own images out of the air
and drop theirs like bombs to the ground. I am lighter
than air. The ground is fear to me.
From up here, I'm just a shade
on the shadow of a tree.

When I am down, my legs pinned,
I roar inside, a lioness
with no claws. It is years later,
this image, the others who have accompanied me

begin their animal walk. I must speak with them
before we are told we are natural enemies.

I will start with you, mother. I have seen you as bird
and lioness too. Bird of prey, eagle, peacock
and battered, winged creature— the weight of your unmet
grace heavy in your broken-boned wings. Then angry,
you enter as cat, your huge paws ripping the grass
as you skim the dry ground. There is dust and the yellow
rush of power. Ears back, you have stopped listening
and attack. You want me to run beside you.

You are an animal who would kill. I have seen your iron
anger, flawless in the heat. There were never any marks,
so it became a question of belief. Trust was a filthy word
to you. A lioness will eat her own legs,
so the cubs can nurse. This is the kind of nurturing
you roared at me. Necessity is ugly, raw and true.

Now Elizabeth, it is you, mourning dove,
I've always felt closest to you.
One day you stood, the next you flew.
You are a seed I caught on the wind accidentally.
My mother told me finally, *you did have an older
sister,* after days and weeks of unconscious pestering.
I asked and asked for an older sister
not knowing you had already come and gone.

A tender cat appears, a mother you knew and I must
too, to see her. She lifts you by your loose-skinned
neck, your heavy head, shoulders you and carries the cloud-
blue eyes to a soft place among the rocks, the other graves
come real. She knew you would be coming here and asked only
that you not be marked, you who were always marked, your
life called impossible beyond the age of six. Enormous head
and downy light brown curls, I heard you whispered, I heard you
from the first, your loyalty as you travelled, always
beside her, hand in hand, a clear signal pressed,
palm to palm, *I love you.*

I wrap myself

in the cellophane, clothes
just back from the dry cleaners—
twirl, enthralled inside
the bubbles. I join and separate
worlds, bunch up corners and trounce
them in an explosive pop,
breaking the film from the inside
out. My mother discovers me,
my held-in air, hand over
her mouth… *Never, never
do that. You could suffocate.*

This is the same room
where he handles me
as I seal off, let my skin
expand to take him in
and let myself out noiselessly
like bubbles breaking
away. You know the crazy dance
of escaping air, the object thrashing
into weightlessness. I am
the air, not the weight. I have
escaped, live outside every room
I enter.

ROOM
for Leslie

I open the door on my old room—
blue covers piled in the center,
windows like two great eyes: equidistant
New England. I sit at my desk, lamp
of worry lighting the late dark,
and press against the windows, my life
as water slapping glass.
The points of the compass lock
in combination: north as always.
So I arrive at the same door,
remember the proud blue veins
of anger stored in the roof.

It is here where you enter
and begin— strong, present
hands tracing the walls.
The stencils of self-doubt quicken
under your touch. Now
you are getting warm.
Yes, I lived here and left,
fled like air past the bubbled glass.
Early America, a line
of waving cut-outs. We are moving by
flooding doors, hands still holding fiercely
as we walk into the room of stars.

Fear's boats have been launched
into the dry light. We follow
in a craft of our own making.
Afloat on the water,
we arrive in the same place:
hands   rooms   full of speech.

FLOWING OUT, AWAY

I remember everything
by myself. Nights
the lights turn up loud
like music. The wicker chair
becomes the one who feels
no love and shines hard
through the white paint.
I converse with it softly   undoing
the weave of hard grasses, the stubbed brass
feet. I am crying for this
formality— these objects
bursting threads in my mind.

CALM EXTERIORS
for Joan

Calm exteriors betray themselves
like my father busy dying,
like my face driving the air
dull around me. The buds pellet down,
stone the storm windows, still on
as we stare outside the frigid
core of my father's air-
conditioned room. Our dumb skins crawl
and wait, the climate breathless, hot or cold.
This is July. It will never rain.

Hoping the hoarse breathing had stilled, I walked
outside on the wet grass, the green watery
lawn soothing my feet and fell weeping
out of earshot, under the apple tree.
I assumed I was alone, that my voice
thinned off and did not pass through the walls
but the walls were membranes and the dying
senses flash out gloriously one by one.
So it must have been: my father's habit
of reading, bathrobed, through the night
brought me into his pages. *Are you all
right?* and the man without breath
or speech came to ask me ever so kindly
back to the house, back to the trusting
walls where osmosis deepened
the summer night rain.

ESPRIT DE CORPS
for Rosa

We speak through the air—
the light rain, the purple
clouds muscling gray and blue
across the sky. We always meet like this,
out in the open. I cannot tell how
the minutes die in front of us—

I remember how you waited
with me in my mother's house.
She was too sick to talk
but we listened from downstairs
as we snapped on
the lights and spoke,
the living room dense
with her... holding on
to each word, her short breath.
She had a small bell by her bed
when she needed something,
and you loved this asking, this
signal between us. I needed
you, the even comfort in your gold
eyes, telling stories of never, always.

It is a wonder we are still alive.
Every day, a singing, a sign
given against the slow alarm
of life not fully taken.
I hear the rumble of hooves
let go— ringing inside the metals
of the earth, the bright air
flashing, the unearthing
of a life.

ONE TO ONE

I

Our love began 50's-style in a Ford Galaxy—
long wide seats and traditional loveknot,
legs and arms tangled, listening
to the other's news. Every night, the first
summer, slick sides to everything, melons
cantaloupe and honeydew, July's exploding
fireworks reached all the way through August.

You drew my hunger slowly out,
your golden paws expert, letting
tenderness weight the air
to bring my asking to a close.
You pinned my wrists in cool pillows
and rolled over me in a wave.

II

We passed The Countryview late that fall—
it was there the engine rattled, backfired and blew.
The nearest farmhouse, Milton's Hilton, New Yorkers
moved north: The Wife set jeering The Game
from her chair, the year the Sox came so close.
We lurked in the kitchen el while he
got permission to drive us home, twenty miles
to South Brooksville. *You girls*
don't want to be out in this, the first snow.
We'll see the Ford's off the road, don't want her
catching it with the side of the plow. Nice-looking
body, she's worth something sure. The old tortoise
shell grown slow in winter. We
heaved into bed, posts centered in that cold,
third-floor room and heaped up new walls
with the old quilts, let frost come
white onto the inside panes. Slow paling
of our bodies, just a form of hiding,
when winter presses the blood further in.

III

Confusion burrows in and marks the food, bed,
music, the personalities we keep

whose changing touch and mouthing silences
iron moods in and out of our clothes.
This year, the spring lets us out
into the City and we are on the run,
our shadows the first to feel
the sorrow ahead. I do not look
for magnet sameness
but seek the ragged river, flashing forks
where we diverge—
not name it Plattsburgh on the map
but how to reach through spooling falls,
from inside walls, what landscape stops the eye,
mica chips embedded in your gaze.

IV

You're driving out Long Island tonight.
This is where you grew up, where the orchards
were, a few isolated oaks and new brick
schools. Your mother's bottles
leaked poison to the street—
slamming windows and pulling shades, you
whispered fiercely at the neighbors from the cracks,
Get out of here if you know what's good for you.
The bitter gossip hushed like a quiet self-hatred.
You poured and poured the golden braids of Scotch
down the drain and hid the new ones just delivered
to the front door. When the doorbell rang, you unsnapped
your mother's purse and paid. The nickels and lipstick
stuck with tobacco flakes. You wanted
no more money in your hands.

You are driving out Long Island tonight
making no waves, while inside, the child
says, *Take me with you, take me away*—
no doors, no answers—*Let me come
home* and find my body.

It was a red umbrella

firing the gray tumble,
the heavy cloudshrug.

What a weekend!
No picnic— the child under
the kitchen table, body braced
for approaching footsteps, the hands she knew
so well across her small, caged back.
Chin down, she kept her face away.
After all, there was school
the next day. And being let out to play.

It was the neighbor
coming to freshen her tea
as the child curled tight under the table.
It was the child who saw the neighbor's
easy, brown shoes,
knew she'd made a mistake
and unfurled her best
improvisation: *I'm trying somersaults!*
then took the hands that pulled
her out— through the hoops of dread,
words that broke up in her mouth.
From the center of the kitchen stage
the child opened a red umbrella—
It will protect me from the sky.
There's a fire in here no one sees but me.

This child was not the ideal
witness. She missed details,
waved surrender with blank sheets—
no memory, a stream of jokes
and how she said at night
she felt all windy inside.

CONVERSATION WITH THE BODY

My sex opens like a fan: thigh, thigh, thigh—
bones like rays elongate; the breath

lights the fingers, the palms blink open
and listen to the air. The body swims
after it— out of breath.

No one is here beside me—
just the suspended questions
that shine— asking
how to touch. I hear
answering all along my spine. Stars
flex in the high hum of the dark.

I've broken out of expectations,
don't look for a lover
and yet, at first, inspect everything—
grumpy, kicking the newly empty
boxes around the rooms without
doors where the unexpected
moves ahead of me.

I'm talking now— taking my body
for a ride in the atmosphere   having
volcanoed out, spit rock from my stone lap,
violet-red pebble rage.
I inhabit the soft-hair surfaces,
hot-pulse the air
marking space like the tiger
in the tiger coat.

What is it, my hands could
almost touch? Open, unready,
not lost or waiting... this
body and no other.

WILD BLUE

My rich cloudbank with the many blue backs—
boneless, beautiful disaster— so tired of this
present, the purple dust I face,
constant in my eyes; sunsets and proud moonlight
I am always covering. What's inside,
oh wild blue confusion: moisture clinging
to the dust of the universe. I come from

everywhere with no place to go.
How to feel welcome next to the bright, hard
metal of stars. My absence is considered
a miracle on cloudless days. I rest
dissipated, fallen into snow, condensation
to the garden stirring out of the ground.

Anything is possible.
Even secrets, hinged like dark blue shells
grown under the coldest waters,
release: spin fire to the surface,
break skyward and open to the world,
dizzy into the light: wild blue
telling all in calm freefall
before disappearing like skywriting.

CHANGING PLACES
for Jean

Who is this stranger?
She is lighter than the other
characters I keep and walks towards me—
arms, a smile— I know you,
wordless, amused and then outloud,
Tell me anything. I've never heard
from you and I've been here.
She seems to have the laughter to prove it—
ragged, deep, changing places.

Take this bowl of years,
light shell, unblurred by partial text.
The din you were afraid had no place to go
but wounded, further in.
Out the angry head, flame
stutterer has more to say.

Music could burn down the house:
red hair, blue eyes—
my mother, the source.

Sorrow cup
how well you hold the sun.
Pounding bass   glory's hay head
Do not leave yourself
alone. Toll the bright echo,
far-seeing necessity.

Stranger cups my head in her hands
hears how close I've been.

III

TRIPTYCH
for Ron King, Lynnsey Carroll and Tracy Sampson

I: RON

Charlie said he wanted to die
and Dell and I were the ones,
of course, who were going to
help him do it. You know Dell—
Charlie's ex, most recent
ex. Well, the exes were
elected, me and Dell.
No one in the family
was going to do it, and Charlie said
he was ready this time. You know last
summer he almost died, we had
bedside vigils, the whole bit, then he
felt better and went to Florida
for the winter. Stayed in the trailer park
with his brother, Dirk. Yeah, that's right,
same time that I broke my leg,
six foot four inch faggot in a cast
and Charlie was feeling okay then
so he rode me all around the fucking
trailer park on that giant
tricycle. What a picture.
Anyway, Charlie was ready to die,
so we did all the preparation,
read the book by what's-his-name—
Humphries— got the pills.
Everyone knew, the family
was supportive. None of them
wanted to *be there*, but they were ready
because Charlie was ready. They all
came and said their goodbyes, so Dell and I
go over to Charlie's house on Saturday night
with all the stuff expecting to wake up
with Charlie dead. All three of us—

Dell, Charlie and me— had read the instructions
five or six times each, of course, but we
were nervous as shit. The pills are supposed to
work better with alcohol, so I had

some Scotch ready. He wouldn't take it.
He was adamant, he wouldn't touch the
stuff, said it had been hard enough
to get sober and stay sober. He insisted
on water, even though I begged
him. I told him it didn't make any
difference. He wanted to go out
sober though. So I gave him the pills—
with water. He had stopped eating— was just
taking fluids, so swallowing the pills
wasn't easy. He took every
one of those suckers, ten of them,
drank them down one at a time, thanked me
and lay down. We waited, set beside him
for two hours, then went in the other
room. Dell lay down and I set the clock,
just in case, but I couldn't sleep at all,
of course. Got up at 2, went and checked
on him, he was still breathing,
the fucker, so I went back
and told Dell, who was wide awake,
that he was still alive.

I got up again at a little after 3, looked
in and his chest wasn't moving. I was sure
this was it. I woke
Dell up, told him Charlie had
stopped breathing. I'd promised
to call Charlie's brother, Dirk,
yeah, the straight one, the one closest
to him, and there was Sue, a really close
woman friend from the program. She
said she wanted to know when he died. So I called
Dirk's and got his machine. Couldn't deal
with that so I hung up. I got
Sue and she thanked me. I sat down and had
a cigarette when Dell came back in the room,
and said he had closed Charlie's eyes.
I shrieked, "You what? His eyes weren't
open when I was in there." We ran
back and took his pulse. It was
going. The fucker was still alive
and I swear he wasn't breathing when I was

in there. We didn't know what to do, felt
guilty as hell that we'd failed him,
went in the kitchen to talk and have more
cigarettes. We found a garbage bag
in there and decided to try
and smother him. So there's Dell and me,
scared to death, creeping up either side
of the bed, ready to pull this bag
over his head and hold him down if he
struggles. What a picture we must've made.
We're just ready to slip the bag
over his head and his eyes pop open.
We just couldn't do it: pull a bag over a man's
head with him staring at us. We left
the room and talked and talked,
harangued over not doing
our job, about failing him,
and finally, thank God, we realized we'd done
enough, that it wasn't our job to do
anymore. It was his job and he'd have to
do it himself if he wanted to die.
I had to call Sue back
and tell her Charlie was not dead.

I am exhausted waiting
for Charlie to die. I feel this
incredible weight but I just can't
do anything more about it. This week
I realized the fucker repeated
the same thing that happened
over and over in our relationship. I'd get
all the information, try to do it
all for him, and he wouldn't be ready.
Then when I'd just about given up, he'd go
do it himself. Well, this is something
I can't do for him. I love him
but he's just going to have to die himself.

II: CATHY

Well, since I became a lesbian...
You mean last week, Lynnsey
interrupts laughing. We all

laugh, glad to, after Charlie's
funeral, laughing at how much is
possible after all. Cathy
leaps ahead headlong, Yeah, well,
it's been three weeks, actually.
I'll tell you my life has really
changed. Being HIV Positive
is nothing compared to this.
Course I can't stop talking
about it and you know, not
everyone wants to hear about it either.
This gets a big laugh from back and front
seat. And you people, well my God,
I've got four dykes
right here in one car.
I have to hear all
about how you met, you know,
how you got together.
I don't know what I'm doing.
I've been talking
about it in my meetings
but they think they've heard enough,
what with me being HIV Positive
and all, they don't want to hear
about my being a lesbian too.
They've been through Harry,
my ex-lover dying from AIDS, two
years now it's been, and my ex-
husband and his being positive
now too. You just don't know.
Now my ex-husband, he's
great about my being a lesbian. He's not
threatened or anything. And my support
group in Bangor, they're good,
and of course, the gay/lesbian meeting, but
I need to talk about this a lot
and my regular AA home group
in Bangor, well, one of them,
I thought she was my friend, she says
to me, Cathy it's too much. We're just
here to talk about problems of alcoholism.
We heard all about Harry's IV drug use

and your HIV, but this is too much.
They think it's a tragedy. She doesn't
understand that I'm happier
than I've ever been in my whole entire
life. After thirty-two years, I am finally
in the right place at the right time.
I'm fine. I don't want to drink. Another thing,
a lot of straight people, they think
if I've said it out loud
once, I should be done.
They don't understand this being
a lesbian changes everything in my life.
Everything. I barely know
what to say anymore, I want
to tell everyone of course, my family
and my old friends from school but I can
see from the reaction at meetings
that I'm going to have to be more
selective, pick and choose who
I talk to because I don't need
any shit about this— like I said,
this is the best thing that ever
happened to me. And it *is* related
to my sobriety, goddammit. If I wasn't
sober, I wouldn't know how to think
over anything. I was hiding
all the time, drowning in booze.
Now I'm making some real
choices and I'm pleased as punch
about it. I listen to everyone
else tell about their relationships—
wives, weddings, bosses, you name it.
I don't complain. I get something
out of it. Well, they should
be able to, too. It's crazy.
They haven't heard near
enough from me. Why
shouldn't I be able to talk
about being lesbian?
It's good for 'em
to see there are other ways
of loving. My ex-husband,

he understands no problem.
He's one of my best friends. He
called in the middle of the night, the other
night. He was freaking out—
not about me— about being Positive
now too— and he couldn't think of anyone
else to call. What guy can he call?
Guys don't talk to guys, at least not straight
ones. He doesn't have any supports yet, it's so new.
He kept apologizing for calling
but he really didn't know
who else to call. So I talked with him
for awhile, calmed him down
some, told him it was a big
adjustment and he didn't have to
do it alone, that there were
all kinds of supports now— thanks
to you Lynnsey and you Tracy.
I told him how 2 lesbians started
Downeast AIDS Network and got the guys,
the political ones, working too,
and how you worked with the state
agencies and got grants, how you
started it all in your own home,
had the office on the stairs
and how D.E.A.N. had a big office now
and two paid positions, all because
you just fucking did it, organized
it right here in downeast Maine.
I told him how it was for lovers
and family members, for straight
people too. I gave him
the whole nine yards. I told him he can go
to the support group like I did—
get mad, talk about it,
let it out, and eventually he'd
maybe get to where he could accept
it and get on with his
life. You know it makes you
think. I didn't paint too rosy
a picture for him. The anger, grief
and pain all come back, after all

we're only human. But he can
find people, good ones
he can trust, then
get on with it, the way
I have. Anyway, he said he felt
a lot better and thanked me
and said 'God bless 'em' about
you Lynnsey and you Tracy.
He'll be all right. I know
he will. But I got to meet
some women. I need to hear
all I can to get ready.
Now Lynnsey and Tracy, you met here in Maine,
right? So there's hope for me.
I need to hear all
about it, everything. Then
we can move on to you Bea
and you Roz. You're from another
country. I'd like to hear about that.
Hell, maybe I should come down
to New York and meet some women.

III: HOMELESS

Morning sun outside D'Agostino's, a young man bends,
crooked towards a parked car, heavy brown
raincoat, denim jeans and white shirt.
Smooth face, dark brown beard, hair shiny
in gentle curls away from his face.
His skin: translucent, taut across the bones
in his face, pink cheeks. His brow: a dome
over liquid brown eyes, deep-set under dark
eyebrows, long lashes. In one hand, he clasps
a sheaf of papers, his fingers curled.
He holds the papers up, shield at shoulder-height.
"Excuse me, I need help."
I walk towards him, he's not
threatening. I see his physical
weakness. "I was in a hotel," he says, "I was robbed,
they beat me up," I see the bruise on the side of his face
and look again into his eyes. I stop,
rest my bags at my feet. "It's dangerous
now," he continues, "it's no good anymore. They ruined it.

The addicts. They steal everything. They stole
my money, my medicine, my AZT. They sell it on the street."
His eyes start to brim, "I get my check this week, see"
he holds the papers towards me, "see, here's my ID,
here're my papers. See, it's me." The tiny square
snapshot shows a large head, shorn.
I tell him to hold onto his
papers. I don't need to see
them. I ask if he's been to GMHC. "Yeah,
they got me a place, at the AIDS Hospice,"
he gestures down the street towards Christopher.
"GMHC only takes people under $5000, my checks put me over,
but they got me a referral to the hospice." He stops,
eyes brimming again, "I'm sorry," he looks down, shifts
his weight, stumbles in the space between the car
and the curb, touches my arm inadvertently, draws back
fast, "I didn't mean to touch you, I'm
sorry." "It's OK," I steady his elbow. "I'm so tired,"
he leans against the brown coupe outside the French restaurant.
"What do you need?" "I'm so ashamed, I hate asking
for anything. I ate out of a garbage can this morning.
I never did that before. I ate someone's leftover McDonald's."
"It's OK, you were hungry, you got some food."
He begins to cry, then stops, "I'm gay, my father,"
he's Italian, he's homophobic. He won't help me,
he disowned me, my father. He's so sick,
he doesn't understand, he's so sick, my father."
"What's your name?" I ask. "What do you need?"
"I'm so ashamed for asking like this,
I just have to. I got to get to the MacBurney Y,
they have a room for one night they said,
if I get up there. I need to rest. I have lesions,
on my legs," he pats his blue-jeaned thighs,
"they get infected, I got to clean them out, get
some peroxide." I know I have money
in my pocket, thirty dollars in the bank.
I reach in my pocket, pull out a ten-
dollar bill, direct him, "Go out to Hudson, you know
the park…" "I need to sit down," he interrupts, "I'm so tired…"
"You know the benches, you can sit down and rest
on one of the benches down the street by the laundromat.
When you're ready, get a cab

on 8th Avenue. It'll take you right up
to the Y." I have never given anyone
a ten-dollar bill on the street before. "I can get your address
and pay you back, I get my check next week." "Forget it,
go sit down, go to the Y, sleep, rest." "I can't thank
you enough. Bless you, thank you," he crosses Greenwich
towards Hudson. I turn, my hands barely able to grasp
the two bags of groceries, lift the weight,
carry them around the corner.
I turn, see the back of his
raincoat, the beautiful chestnut curls
over his collar.

Next week, I am headed to the bank
to deposit a check. I am celebrating
inside, Thank God! Down to my last two dollars. Right outside
the bank, I see him at the corner of 8th
and West 12th in his raincoat talking
with a young woman clearly on her way to work.
She is gesturing, "Go to the Center, the Gay/Lesbian
Center on West 13th St.," she is overpronouncing
her words. He is repeating, "the Center, the Center"
as if he has never heard of it. I pass them
quickly, fury carrying me into the bank.
Lying son of a bitch, goddam faggot, draining off women's
energy, lesbian energy like no one
ever dies from anything besides AIDS. Community,
my ass. How many faggots are nursing women
with breast cancer or anything else for that matter.
All he had to do was get to the fucking
YMCA. It didn't happen, goddam liar.
I make out my deposit slip, fill in
the date, bank account #, the deposit for $357,
sign my name. I decide to confront him
when I'm done, if he's still out there. *Remember me*
I'll say, *What happened to my*
ten dollars, you son of a bitch?
I pad quickly over to the express
deposit, put in my bank card,
check my balance:— $10.50. Shit, what happened?
I seal the envelope, pop it
in the slot, punch in the envelope number
and it drops safely in.

Get the deposit slip, $2 till tomorrow— $1
for milk, 65¢ for a cup in the morning, 35¢
for NEWSDAY, and by 3 the check will be clear.
Minus $10.50, what happened?
Christ, who knows. At least I got
paid, I'll be OK.

Outside, the corner is empty, swept clear, a short
line to the ATM. *Remember me*
Maybe he wouldn't remember, maybe
he couldn't remember...
Why didn't he know The Center?
I begin to choke on my own breath
as I realize he may not remember.
AIDS in the last stages.
Is he lying or not remembering?
Is he dying or running a scam
or both? Does he know the difference? Do I?
Do I need or deserve to know
because I gave him $10, because
I'm a lesbian who has seen too
much of this disease?
Anything could have happened.
We live in New York City.
I wanted it to be simple: cross
the street, go sit down, rest,
get the cab uptown, then sleep.
In the morning breakfast,
take a cab to the AIDS
hospice. Here he enters the place where
he will die. I want to know
I have finished. But he has not
arrived anywhere. I bumped into him,
the motion of his life down the street.
He showed me that it was the world,
not he himself alone who held
his body in his hands.

REFUGE

I

All day it snowed and we bore further into it— no visible progress, a hot core
of comfort in the warm car— hot feet, radio and you dozing off as I peered into
the unseeable spinning wind. Blizzard conditions. Next day, in the deep quiet
of the snow, we walked the road to the nature preserve, cut across the open
slope, the sky's crackling blue above us.

We waded through the deep surrounding
snow: my thighs burned in the cold soft parting
Hands hooked on my waistband
you pull me from behind: I turn easy
as a spool of lavender-shaded twine
in your hands, stand in the
enlarged silence as you secure expectation— -
I want you here—
take off your coat and kneel to lay it down
in the fresh path my legs have made before you

II

Looking up   your face changing fast
full of what you want
we have met in the shaking space
inside the snow globe   all desire
water around us   snow loose on the ground
ready to be shaken   to be touched
stripping the cover from the hot cold
quivering hillside   my skin gold
against the snow

No cold or words between us
your hands know what they want   unzip my pants
enough to thread folded fingers
between my thighs   Heated soft, I sit quietly on your slowly
turning hand   receiving brushed-bone-sensitive
jumping pulses   I hold your shoulders   raise up
my breasts seeing what they want against the cloth:
shirt buttons in your teeth   soft blue
cotton damp from your tongue   nipples seeking
the eyelet of your open mouth and the talking back:
get serious   don't let go   keep me shaking

your mouth the only hold on what I want
I fall back on my heels   want to stay
standing   want to let you
drive me crazy before wanting to
let you drive me there

III

We climb the crest of the hill to the summer
house   stand looking out at our abandoned
trail   sex angels in the snow   bodies still warm and finding
new outlines in the sun   the whole porch, a sudden open prow,
wood warm to the touch   We say nothing
sun catching us still open to sex
but take it in: the whole porch facing south
minds ticking over everything we might want to do
in this freeing blue unusual air
I move back against the broad wall of the house
hot ribbed shingles under my palms
lancing eyes as this time you drop in front of me
open my loosened jeans and place your whole mouth
fast on my cunt   Head-back held   you are deep under now
calling for light as you begin to swim through me
My hands knead your jaw as I unmoor and go
Sun in your mouth
I am no longer any one fire

IV

We waded through the snow/ our bodies sudden, weighted against the infinite
cold/ sky ripped wide to hot sun/ throwing our bodies forward into the curve
of the hillside/ churning water down the iced cove/ salt gleaming on the
glacier's broken dark gold rocks/ shattered motion of sea further out/ I begin to
run by falling forward/ thighs burning as I part the snow/ jagged softness/
reach a shallow cradle in the slope and gaining/ you pull me back against your
vest/ wrap me in your coat/ *I want you right here*/ Full mouth over-the-shoulder
kiss/ You peel down quickly/ your coat, a raft in the snow/ desire speeding
your efficiency/ I watch in studied patience to slow your every ardent move/
determined to break open all the space we need/ Coat lies peaceful, teasing,
smoothed over our tracks/ You fall forward even as you are pulling me down
by the belt loops/ *right now*/ on my knees.

V

This is the last winter the house will stand.
In the spring it will be destroyed.
Perhaps this is what the old woman meant
when she left the codicile to her will:
when I die, tear the house down,
burn what remains and leave
the land forever wild.

IV

CALL

What was that younger force
made solely in opposition?
—or so I thought.

You taught me
to rake anger to make meaning jump,
how anger had a yearning
and came to listen
then asked the next hard question.

You taught exactitude
using silence
slicing the air
cutting words
into shining —
I use it all.

The wall is gone
the stone-for-stone fear,
wall of revenge,
patient, passionate,
empty. I take it down
stone for stone
ask for fire instead.
I have paid the price of the stone song.

I call you
and ask for fire.
It is your nature—-
fast-moving, frightening.
These days you give it back
without question
pure burning   committed hunger
free for the asking.

We could have been friends in your lifetime.
I held the stones
so tight they changed me:
I love women.
Open-handed,
I take in who you are
thank you.

Granite inside curve of hill—
whose hand, hips house truth?

Sun breaks thunder from winter bones.
We have lived through
enough. I call for fire,
plenty in store,
I call for you.

CROSSING
for Rawn

No wind   and the self pouring down
the smallness   the worry.
I think so little of any of it,
of myself   try to stay open,
hold enough to carry something back.

The boulders bring me to myself
surfacing in smooth cool skin
as they rip the earth wide
and want me crying out for hands.

I want to drag myself up the road
belly open as a great wound,
down through mud and sand.
I call it seeing
when my chest seeks
news of life so violently

but the day is a violent search.

Open a vein
read it
then speak
in the language of slow love

how can you ever say it all
and who can possibly hear it

There is a man here who talks
me back into myself   He is
impossibly sunny and polite,
tells me there has always been

the question of what the white man thinks
but nothing can be done that way
in the bridle of dual consciousness
He says   do whatever you want
then says   I figure I have ten more years

That's when I hear the terrible clarity

MONTAGE
in memory, Richard Lawton

You left in an ambulance
where you studied spring quickly
bleeding by the windows
as you were driven back
to your first home. The barely begun
Maine color, puffs of light
on lavender tips, turns south
to the brightest green entering
and filling all available
openings.

Your lover stayed,
cleaned the shelf cupboard
he'd lined with bulbs, forced
in the dark of January. Narcissus,
hyacinth and crocus stunned the air
as we pulled the rugs from your house
and emptied in a caravan down the drive.

I rode a train,
longed for the moviegoer's view
but nothing had been edited.
You would be the first to die of my friends
from those late seventies.
We moved on at an alarming speed.
I learned to travel with fear
as I visited my mother, her cancer, my father
and his secret. He would die before her.

We slow at your station.
Two conductors take their leave.
Mysterious and official, they walk to the gate,
say goodbye and pivot on their heels.
As we pull away from Providence,
I see the torn life that rests with me,
quickly finger the curtain of the place
I could not bring myself to go,
even as I grew   to hold the dying others.

Arms of gold, red, brown and black,

11/17/93, for Barbara

Audre prepared a nest for you, a warrior's
woven offering— weft facing outward, weave
laid bright over curling boughs— a strong, sheltered space,
rough as bark's protection,
flexible as sap gathered
tight in heart wood. Audre carried you
into New York City where you came to confer
on how best to mark her passing.

I saw Audre
in the elevator, head bound, riding
in full African dress and telling me—
I'll take care of this, *for Barbara*.
The doors closed and she ascended
with a small bow of recognition
towards what was needed at the time.

Bones bitten with loss,
you jumped in front of a cab to stop it.

She said, "Don't freeze to death,"
and you, "I *am* freezing to death."

And what could we do
together? Audre always asked, Audre the one
who slipped through the universe, shot heat
boldly from her center, fully, careful to touch
the crown of your head, and encircle
you, an African-American Lesbian— still standing,
more alone. She bore your weight,
stood by, carefully marking
this time in shadow, the situation turning— the power
of loving clear. Taking on some
of what had passed between you, seeing more
clearly what would be asked for in the days ahead:

I was frightened for you
and let my bones lengthen into it.

BLUE PLACE
for Eva, Jane and Grace

Last beach flowers: the color of asters, old bruised heart
suddenly out on a stalk blooming...
Light is always the first to know
as if the condition of the world
rested on each morning eyelid, dawn slowly spinning
out of view. So what's left for us
here by the edge of the sea where sails clog
what looks like the horizon.

Sunrise has rolled back into the pink glow
of the head of the globe   What did we know?
We didn't know the words
and was there music   another land?
Countries listed off the map   beaches sandpapered
the air and the sea deep-lunged at us
across the tearing edges   Oh forgetful sun
moon and stars   out and shining
bareheaded in weather like this. It couldn't be
time to wake up: head bent with the weight
of startled voices   listening
to the end of dreaming and fighting to be heard.
Memory will not follow
tickle us or age   Only the enormous
accuracy of silence will imprint
our past   a soundless kiss on the lips   goodbye.

My hands fall easily into the hands of women
who stay each other   arms and whole bodies of tenderness
pass into this future with the aroma of suicide
salt in the air   in our mouths.
We move out from the blue
place   this palpable hurt on earth.
The sense of it: pain
but not blindness. No.

POND

I loved you as if we had touched
the billowing air that spun our fresh-mown
thoughts: heady August, your amber eyes like rays.
Leonine, you watched me: deeply shaded and alone.
I loved the sparks of grass, pale green and blonde,
flung wide as you rolled down the length of lawn.
We walked the steep, damp path to the pond,
divided the surface into lines on the face
of difference, the softening creases
around your joints, my large hope like the water between us.
Gray head tipped water-dark, I watched
you go and swam hard into acceptance
wanting exhaustion and a map for distance.
I loved you as if we had touched.

23RD STREET CINEPLEX

Denis's eyes clear blue and bright,
his body a wand.
—How are you?— and I see
his pupils glare
—I'm in a rage. Everything,
just everything—
—What's going on?—
—I want to live—
The words flare, drop
on the sidewalk, then curl
in charcoal at our feet

I hold Denis tight in my gaze
as we ripple together
in the brutal spring tide
of fresh river scent.
I hold the daily forms of rupture
tenderly, new to the spider's
art, the web of spit
and long drop from center.

Is it his death or mine
standing beside us   camouflaged as one
waiting casually for another
as our bones point with murderous urban
accuracy to the theatre entrance.

DREAM: BAY FOAL
for Roz

I was given a beauty
wide sweet head
and I rubbed her right
between the eyes.
She pressed hard
against my palm. She adored
me. Soft gray eyelids, nostrils
of the same smokey flesh.
Velvet mouth and nose
whiskers.

She curled, all legs, in my lap
her hooves held high
in the air   dark horn
tips   from the rippling basket
of limbs she formed
in my arms: A love.

The muscles in her flanks
liquid as I stroked
and rubbed her down.
Her new bones turned easy
muscles gliding between
my fingers, almost fingers themselves,
the deep pleasure pushing back
the chords of power
under her beautiful brown
skin. This cannot keep
up   I thought   the first cold
to enter the dream.

Full gaze.
She turned her muscled neck
thick shiny chestnut
then nibbled   sucking, pulling
on all my fingers
in twos and threes.

To think I almost gave
the foal away
to play with a braid
of wind and cold
and doubt.

PRAISE FOR THE A TRAIN
for Electa

I sit down beside the song, the woman
singing straight ahead, her needles
at work crocheting shawl,
slow mountain rising across her lap.
Her voice makes me open, porous, hungry.
Not seeing but believing, I close my eyes,
the train filling in bright air,
longing safe in the shawl of comfort she is
stitching in and around us. We need her.
She doesn't care. We lean out into the tunnel,
bright sail before her song— rapt, loyal,
forgetting any danger. Sailing underground on steel wheels,
the blue "A", the signal of our naked happiness.
We lay down all our resistances,
surrender to the voice of a woman
becoming the song of our train.

NEGOTIATIONS
for my parents

1

She called in the morning
to tell me, "This is the day,
he's going today." "All right"
I said or something—
I don't remember
asking anything at all
but I took in the trance-like
assuredness of her voice
accepting it fully
like breath
and joined her in the aloneness…
even as I hated the telephone
in my hand, the voice in my throat
and the distance closing.
I touched the hot cold
let my father   dying
in close   ears open   hearing
nothing more from him.

It was as she wanted
and I could only guess
he too wanted
The intensity
of her voice seemed to speak
to the approach   She was ready
to give him over
even as she counted,
heart beating in the stone-lined well,
the moments alive before her.
No fear allayed, she refused
to negotiate beyond
what was essential
"I just wanted to tell you,"
she said   her voice holding
all the proprietary calm
and fear of her solo watch
meeting the raw
truth of it
as usual.

~

Later telling me she thought
it was odd, when he packed
all his clothes for just a month
in the country, adding "I didn't say
anything." She didn't feel the
air leaving his lungs and
not coming back, at least
not then   Or the tightness
of his chest and shoulders
as he felt all his suits
and shoes slowly filling
with strangers
and walking away.

2

What strikes me now is
the weight behind the words—
her saying, "I knew he was gone
when he hit the floor."
"What happened?" I asked.
"He fell out of bed."
She was there
in the same room
in the chair I had struggled
to speak from weeks before

as I sat trying to tell my father
the news of my life
the desires I had,
going back to school
and not knowing how to tell
him the clear facts of my life—
how much I loved him
and counted him the source
and foundation of any sanity,
gentleness or hope I had been able
to hold— It was so simple.
I wanted to echo his greeting of the world,
but I wasn't as good,
prone to prideful resistance and fear,
I held on

~

I didn't hide
and I didn't speak,
the desire alive
the wordlessness
still and large— his sweet, interested face
craning forward, small breath
deepened by the line of oxygen
piped from the portable tanks

His own words had to be short,
his breath couldn't carry them,
so the words must have
started to accumulate
and then fallen
like stones in a crumbling well—
a few more falling each day
loosening the earth on the way down
until the depth of desire
could not be measured nor
the thousand expressions of it—
but the stones became the love
of holding the words inside
until they are just
the right ones
and match the conditions
perfectly— even the changing
and laughing, that kind of fluidity
and grace—

so when he fell,
he weighed every word
and then toppled, stone falling
before the open mouth of water

He fell beside my mother,
his witness, who had heard it all
before, but jumped up from the
listening chair, quick crouch,
alight in all the sounds
this body can utter.

Beatrix Gates has published two books of poetry, *Shooting at Night* and *native tongue*, and edited *The Wild Good: Lesbian Photography & Writings on Love*. Her work has appeared in many places including *The Kenyon Review Theatre Issue*, *The Nation* and *Gay & Lesbian Poetry in Our Time*. For three years she organized the Poetry Series at A Different Light Bookstore. As founder of Granite Press, she published letterpress editions and trade paperbacks of poetry. She also served on the Kitchen Table: Women of Color Press Transition Team. A graduate of the MFA Program of Sarah Lawrence College, she has had residencies at The MacDowell Colony and The Millay Colony. She has taught at Hampshire College, Goddard College and The New School for Social Research and is currently teaching at New York University. She lives in Greenport, New York.